EMMANUEL JOSEPH

The Canvas of the Mind, How Psychology and Ecology Shape Artistic Expression

*Copyright © 2025 by Emmanuel Joseph*

*All rights reserved. No part of this publication may be reproduced, stored or transmitted in any form or by any means, electronic, mechanical, photocopying, recording, scanning, or otherwise without written permission from the publisher. It is illegal to copy this book, post it to a website, or distribute it by any other means without permission.*

*First edition*

*This book was professionally typeset on Reedsy. Find out more at reedsy.com*

# Contents

| | | |
|---|---|---|
| 1 | Chapter 1: The Dawn of Artistic Expression | 1 |
| 2 | Chapter 2: The Psychological Foundations of Creativity | 3 |
| 3 | Chapter 3: The Role of Nature in Artistic Inspiration | 5 |
| 4 | Chapter 4: Cultural Influences on Artistic Expression | 7 |
| 5 | Chapter 5: The Evolution of Artistic Techniques and Mediums | 9 |
| 6 | Chapter 6: The Intersection of Art and Science | 11 |
| 7 | Chapter 7: The Influence of Technology on Art | 13 |
| 8 | Chapter 8: The Role of Art in Social Change | 16 |
| 9 | Chapter 9: The Psychological Impact of Art on the Viewer | 18 |
| 10 | Chapter 10: The Artist's Journey: From Inspiration to... | 20 |
| 11 | Chapter 11: The Future of Art and Artistic Expression | 23 |
| 12 | Chapter 12: The Eternal Dance of Psychology and Ecology in... | 25 |

# 1

# Chapter 1: The Dawn of Artistic Expression

A rt has always been a reflection of human experience, a mirror held up to nature, society, and the inner workings of the mind. From the earliest cave paintings to contemporary digital art, the evolution of artistic expression is intertwined with the development of human consciousness. In this chapter, we will explore the origins of art and how early humans used it as a tool for survival, communication, and community bonding.

**The First Artists and Their World** Imagine the first artist, hunched over a rock canvas, depicting a successful hunt or a vivid dream. These early artworks were more than mere decoration; they were a means of making sense of the world and sharing that understanding with others. In the harsh and unpredictable environment of early human life, art served as a way to preserve knowledge, celebrate achievements, and foster a sense of community.

**Art as a Survival Tool** Art played a crucial role in early human survival. Depictions of animals and hunting scenes not only recorded successful hunts but also served as educational tools for future generations. By studying these images, young hunters could learn about animal behavior, hunting techniques, and the geography of their surroundings. In this way, art became a vital means of passing down essential survival knowledge.

**The Role of Ritual and Symbolism** Early art was deeply intertwined with ritual and symbolism. Cave paintings often depicted not only animals and human figures but also abstract symbols and patterns. These symbols had significant meaning within the context of early human societies, serving as markers of important events, spiritual beliefs, and social hierarchies. Through art, early humans could communicate complex ideas and emotions that went beyond the limitations of spoken language.

**Community and Communication** Art also served as a powerful tool for community bonding. By gathering together to create and admire art, early humans could strengthen social ties and foster a sense of shared identity. The act of creating art was often a communal activity, with multiple individuals contributing to a single work. This collaborative process not only allowed for the exchange of ideas and skills but also reinforced the social cohesion necessary for survival in a challenging environment.

**A Window into the Past** Today, the art of early humans provides us with a fascinating window into their world. By studying these ancient artworks, we can gain insights into the lives, beliefs, and experiences of our ancestors. From the majestic cave paintings of Lascaux to the enigmatic petroglyphs of the American Southwest, the art of early humans continues to captivate and inspire us, reminding us of our shared heritage and the enduring power of artistic expression.

# 2

# Chapter 2: The Psychological Foundations of Creativity

At the heart of artistic expression lies the human mind, a complex and mysterious organ capable of extraordinary creativity. This chapter delves into the psychological underpinnings of creativity, examining theories from Freud's concept of the unconscious to modern understandings of cognitive processes.

**Freud's Unconscious Mind** Sigmund Freud, the father of psychoanalysis, proposed that much of our creativity stems from the unconscious mind. According to Freud, the unconscious is a reservoir of thoughts, memories, and desires that lie beneath the surface of conscious awareness. Artistic expression, in Freud's view, is a way of bringing these hidden elements to light. Through techniques such as free association and dream analysis, Freud sought to uncover the unconscious motivations behind artistic creation.

**Cognitive Processes and Creativity** Modern psychology offers a different perspective on creativity, focusing on the cognitive processes that drive artistic expression. Researchers have identified several key cognitive functions involved in creativity, including divergent thinking, pattern recognition, and problem-solving. Divergent thinking, for example, involves generating multiple ideas or solutions from a single starting point, while pattern recognition allows artists to identify and manipulate recurring themes and motifs in their work.

**Emotions and Memories as Creative Fuel** Emotions and memories play a crucial role in the creative process. Artists often draw on their personal experiences and emotional states to create works that resonate with viewers. By channeling their feelings and memories into their art, they can convey complex emotions and tell compelling stories that might be difficult to express through words alone. This emotional depth adds a layer of authenticity and relatability to their work, making it more impactful and engaging.

**Art as Therapy** Art can also serve as a therapeutic outlet for expressing feelings that words cannot capture. Art therapy, a form of psychotherapy that uses artistic expression to address psychological issues, has gained recognition as an effective treatment for a wide range of mental health conditions. By creating art in a supportive and non-judgmental environment, individuals can explore their thoughts and emotions, gain insights into their experiences, and develop healthier coping mechanisms.

**The Dance Between Conscious and Subconscious** The creative process is often described as a dance between the conscious and subconscious mind. While the conscious mind sets goals, makes decisions, and plans actions, the subconscious mind generates ideas, forms associations, and taps into emotions. This interplay between the two levels of consciousness allows artists to access a wealth of inspiration and produce work that is both original and deeply meaningful.

# 3

# Chapter 3: The Role of Nature in Artistic Inspiration

Nature has always been a muse for artists, providing endless sources of beauty, mystery, and wonder. This chapter explores the symbiotic relationship between artists and their natural surroundings, from the tranquil landscapes of the Impressionists to the raw power of Land Art.

**The Beauty of Landscapes** Artists have long been captivated by the beauty of landscapes, seeking to capture the essence of the natural world in their work. The Impressionists, for example, were known for their vibrant depictions of outdoor scenes, using light and color to convey the fleeting impressions of nature. Through their work, they aimed to evoke the emotional experience of being immersed in a natural setting, inviting viewers to share in their sense of wonder and awe.

**Ecosystems and Artistic Styles** Different ecosystems and climates have influenced artistic styles and themes in unique ways. In the lush, verdant landscapes of the tropics, artists often draw inspiration from the vibrant colors and intricate patterns of flora and fauna. In contrast, the stark, arid beauty of desert landscapes can evoke a sense of isolation and introspection, leading artists to explore themes of solitude and resilience. By attuning themselves to their natural surroundings, artists can create work that reflects the unique character of their environment.

**Environmental Changes and Artistic Movements** Environmental changes, such as climate shifts and natural disasters, can also inspire new artistic movements. The rise of Land Art in the 1960s and 1970s, for example, was partly a response to growing environmental awareness and concerns about human impact on the planet. Artists like Robert Smithson and Nancy Holt created large-scale works that engaged directly with the landscape, using natural materials and processes to highlight the interconnectedness of humans and nature. Through their work, they aimed to foster a greater appreciation for the environment and promote sustainable practices.

**Stories of Nature-Inspired Artists** Throughout history, countless artists have drawn their inspiration from the natural world. Consider the story of Vincent van Gogh, who found solace and inspiration in the rural landscapes of southern France. His iconic paintings, such as "Starry Night" and "Sunflowers," are infused with the vivid colors and dynamic forms of nature, reflecting his deep connection to the environment. Similarly, the American painter Georgia O'Keeffe found inspiration in the stark beauty of the New Mexico desert, creating works that celebrate the unique forms and textures of the landscape.

**The Influence of Ecology on Perception** The study of ecology, or the relationships between living organisms and their environment, can also influence the way we perceive and represent the natural world. By understanding the intricate web of connections that sustain life, artists can create work that highlights the interdependence of all living things. This ecological perspective can foster a sense of stewardship and responsibility, encouraging viewers to appreciate and protect the natural world.

# 4

# Chapter 4: Cultural Influences on Artistic Expression

Art is a reflection of the society in which it is created, shaped by cultural norms, values, and traditions. In this chapter, we will examine how different cultures throughout history have influenced artistic expression, from the intricate patterns of Islamic art to the vibrant colors of African tribal masks.

**The Rich Tapestry of Cultural Art** Each culture brings its unique perspective and aesthetic to the world of art. The intricate geometric patterns and calligraphy of Islamic art, for example, reflect the cultural emphasis on symmetry, order, and the beauty of the written word. These artworks often carry deep spiritual significance, serving as a form of devotion and meditation. In contrast, the dynamic and vibrant colors of African tribal masks embody the cultural importance of ritual, storytelling, and community.

**Cultural Exchange and Blending** Cultural exchange has always played a crucial role in the evolution of artistic expression. As societies interact and influence one another, artistic styles and techniques blend, giving rise to new and exciting forms. The Renaissance, for instance, was a period of intense cultural exchange between Europe and the Islamic world, leading to the incorporation of new artistic techniques, such as perspective and chiaroscuro, into European art. This blending of cultures enriched the artistic landscape, fostering innovation and creativity.

**Globalization and Contemporary Art** In the contemporary art world, globalization has further accelerated the blending of artistic styles and influences. Artists today have unprecedented access to a wide range of cultural traditions and artistic practices, allowing them to draw inspiration from diverse sources. This global perspective has led to the emergence of hybrid art forms that transcend traditional cultural boundaries. By embracing the richness of global artistic traditions, contemporary artists can create work that resonates with a wide audience and fosters cross-cultural understanding.

**Stories of Cultural Influence** Consider the story of the Mexican muralist Diego Rivera, whose work was profoundly influenced by his country's history and culture. Rivera's murals, which depict scenes from Mexican life and history, are a vibrant celebration of his cultural heritage. Similarly, the Japanese artist Yayoi Kusama has drawn on traditional Japanese aesthetics and her personal experiences to create her iconic polka-dot installations. These artists, and many others, demonstrate how cultural influences can shape and enrich artistic expression, creating work that is both deeply personal and universally resonant.

**Cultural Preservation Through Art** Art also plays a crucial role in preserving cultural heritage and traditions. In many indigenous communities, art serves as a means of passing down cultural knowledge and values from one generation to the next. Traditional crafts, such as pottery, weaving, and carving, are not only artistic expressions but also vital aspects of cultural identity. By supporting and celebrating these traditional art forms, we can help preserve the diverse cultural tapestry of our world.

**The Impact of Cultural Context** Understanding the cultural context in which art is created allows us to appreciate the deeper meanings and significance behind the work. By considering the historical, social, and cultural factors that influence artistic expression, we can gain a richer understanding of the artwork and its place within the broader cultural narrative. This cultural awareness enhances our ability to connect with and appreciate art from different traditions and backgrounds.

# 5

# Chapter 5: The Evolution of Artistic Techniques and Mediums

The tools and techniques used by artists have evolved dramatically over time, from the simple pigments of prehistoric cave paintings to the advanced digital tools of today. This chapter traces the history of artistic mediums and techniques, highlighting key innovations and their impact on artistic expression.

**Prehistoric Beginnings** In the earliest days of artistic expression, artists used natural pigments, such as ochre and charcoal, to create images on rock surfaces. These simple yet effective materials allowed early humans to document their experiences and communicate with others. The techniques used to apply these pigments, such as brushing, blowing, and engraving, laid the foundation for future artistic innovations.

**Classical Innovations** As civilizations developed, so too did artistic techniques and materials. The ancient Egyptians, for example, developed sophisticated methods for creating vibrant frescoes and intricate jewelry. The Greeks and Romans further advanced the art of sculpture, using marble and bronze to create lifelike representations of the human form. These classical innovations set the stage for the artistic achievements of the Renaissance and beyond.

**The Renaissance and the Birth of Perspective** The Renaissance was a period of extraordinary artistic innovation, driven by a renewed interest in the classical ideals of beauty and proportion. One of the most significant advancements of this era was the development of linear perspective, a technique that allowed artists to create the illusion of depth and space on a flat surface. Pioneered by artists such as Filippo Brunelleschi and Leon Battista Alberti, perspective transformed the way artists approached composition and paved the way for the realistic depictions of the natural world seen in the works of Leonardo da Vinci and Michelangelo.

**The Advent of Modern Art** The 19th and 20th centuries saw the rise of modern art movements that challenged traditional artistic conventions and embraced new techniques and materials. The Impressionists, for example, experimented with loose brushwork and vibrant colors to capture the fleeting effects of light and atmosphere. The advent of photography and later, digital technology, opened up new possibilities for artistic expression, allowing artists to explore new forms and mediums.

**The Digital Age** In the digital age, artists have access to an unprecedented array of tools and techniques. Digital art, virtual reality, and artificial intelligence have expanded the boundaries of what is possible in the art world. Artists can now create immersive experiences, interactive installations, and algorithmically generated works that push the limits of human creativity. These technological advancements continue to shape the future of artistic expression, offering new ways for artists to engage with their audience and explore their creative potential.

# 6

# Chapter 6: The Intersection of Art and Science

Art and science may seem like disparate fields, but they share a common goal: to understand and explain the world around us. This chapter explores the fascinating intersection of art and science, from Leonardo da Vinci's anatomical drawings to contemporary bio-art that incorporates living organisms.

**Leonardo da Vinci: The Artist-Scientist** Leonardo da Vinci is perhaps the most famous example of the intersection of art and science. His detailed anatomical drawings, which were based on meticulous dissections, combined artistic skill with scientific inquiry. Da Vinci's work demonstrated that art could be a powerful tool for exploring and communicating scientific concepts. His ability to bridge the gap between these two disciplines has inspired countless artists and scientists alike.

**Scientific Discoveries and Artistic Expression** Throughout history, scientific discoveries have had a profound impact on artistic expression. The invention of the microscope, for example, revealed a hidden world of microorganisms that inspired intricate and imaginative depictions in art. Similarly, the discovery of new chemical pigments expanded the artist's palette, allowing for the creation of more vibrant and diverse works. By incorporating scientific knowledge into their art, artists can create work that reflects the complexities and wonders of the natural world.

**The Role of Art in Communicating Science** Art can also serve as a powerful medium for communicating scientific ideas to a broader audience. By translating complex concepts into visual and experiential forms, artists can make science more accessible and engaging. This is particularly important in an age where scientific literacy is crucial for addressing global challenges such as climate change and public health. Through their work, artists can inspire curiosity, foster understanding, and spark meaningful conversations about scientific issues.

**Contemporary Bio-Art** Contemporary bio-art, which incorporates living organisms and biological processes into artistic practice, represents a cutting-edge fusion of art and science. Artists like Eduardo Kac and Heather Dewey-Hagborg use biotechnology to create works that explore themes of identity, ethics, and the nature of life itself. By pushing the boundaries of traditional art forms, bio-artists challenge our perceptions of what art can be and invite us to consider the ethical implications of scientific advancements.

**Stories of Art and Science Collaboration** Consider the story of the collaboration between artist Anicka Yi and synthetic biologist Tal Danino. Together, they created a series of artworks that incorporated living bacteria and other microorganisms. By combining Yi's artistic vision with Danino's scientific expertise, they produced visually stunning and thought-provoking pieces that explored the relationship between humans and microorganisms. This collaboration exemplifies the potential for art and science to complement and enhance one another.

# 7

# Chapter 7: The Influence of Technology on Art

Technology has always played a significant role in the development of art, from the invention of the printing press to the advent of digital art. This chapter examines how technological advancements have transformed artistic expression, allowing artists to experiment with new forms and techniques.

**The Printing Press and the Democratization of Art** The invention of the printing press in the 15th century was a revolutionary moment in the history of art. It allowed for the mass production of printed materials, making art and literature more accessible to a wider audience. This democratization of art paved the way for the spread of artistic ideas and styles, fostering greater creativity and innovation. The printing press also enabled the production of illustrated books, prints, and posters, expanding the possibilities for artistic expression.

**Photography and the Birth of Modern Art** The invention of photography in the 19th century had a profound impact on the art world. It challenged traditional notions of representation and prompted artists to explore new ways of seeing and interpreting reality. Photography's ability to capture moments with unprecedented accuracy and detail influenced movements such as Impressionism, which sought to capture the fleeting effects of light and atmosphere. The advent of photography also led to the development of new artistic genres, such as photojournalism and documentary photography.

**Digital Art and New Media** The rise of digital technology has transformed the way artists create and share their work. Digital art encompasses a wide range of practices, including computer-generated imagery, digital painting, and interactive installations. Artists can now manipulate pixels, algorithms, and data to create works that challenge traditional boundaries and engage viewers in new and immersive ways. The internet and social media have also provided platforms for artists to reach global audiences, democratizing the art world and fostering greater connectivity.

**Virtual Reality and Immersive Art** Virtual reality (VR) has opened up new dimensions of artistic expression by creating immersive environments that viewers can explore and interact with. Artists working with VR can construct entire worlds, blurring the lines between art and experience. This technology allows for the creation of multi-sensory installations that engage not only the visual but also the auditory and tactile senses. By immersing viewers in these virtual spaces, artists can create powerful and transformative experiences.

**Artificial Intelligence and Algorithmic Art** Artificial intelligence (AI) is pushing the boundaries of what is possible in the art world. Algorithmic art, which uses AI to generate and manipulate images, patterns, and forms, challenges traditional notions of authorship and creativity. Artists can collaborate with AI to create works that are both unpredictable and deeply innovative. This fusion of human and machine creativity opens up new possibilities for artistic expression and prompts us to reconsider the nature of artistic creation.

**Stories of Technological Innovation** Consider the story of artist Refik Anadol, who uses data and AI to create stunning visual installations. Anadol's works, such as "Melting Memories," use machine learning algorithms to process data from brain scans and translate them into dynamic visual experiences. By harnessing the power of technology, Anadol creates art that is both cutting-edge and deeply evocative, challenging our perceptions of memory and consciousness.

**The Role of Technology in Accessibility** Technology has also played a crucial role in making art more accessible to a wider audience. Digital platforms and social media allow artists to share their work with people around the world, breaking down geographic and economic barriers. Virtual museums and online galleries provide access to art collections that might otherwise be out of reach for many viewers. By democratizing access to art, technology fosters greater cultural exchange and appreciation.

**Ethical Considerations** As technology continues to transform the art world, it also raises important ethical questions. Issues such as data privacy, copyright, and the environmental impact of digital art production must be carefully considered. Artists and technologists must navigate these challenges to ensure that technological advancements are used responsibly and ethically. By engaging in thoughtful dialogue and collaboration, we can harness the power of technology to enrich the art world while addressing its potential pitfalls.

# 8

# Chapter 8: The Role of Art in Social Change

A rt has the power to inspire, provoke, and challenge societal norms, making it a powerful tool for social change. This chapter explores how artists have used their work to address social issues, from civil rights and gender equality to environmental conservation and political activism.

**Art as a Catalyst for Change** Throughout history, artists have used their work to shine a light on social injustices and inspire change. From the powerful anti-war paintings of Picasso's "Guernica" to the vibrant murals of Diego Rivera that celebrate the dignity of labor, art has the ability to convey powerful messages and mobilize people toward action. By addressing pressing social issues, artists can raise awareness, foster empathy, and inspire collective efforts to create a more just and equitable society.

**Civil Rights and Equality** Art has played a significant role in the fight for civil rights and equality. During the Civil Rights Movement in the United States, artists such as Jacob Lawrence and Faith Ringgold created works that depicted the struggles and triumphs of African Americans. These artworks not only documented historical events but also served as powerful symbols of resistance and hope. By giving voice to marginalized communities, artists can challenge systemic oppression and advocate for social justice.

**Environmental Activism** Environmental conservation has become an increasingly urgent issue, and artists have risen to the challenge by creating works that highlight the beauty and fragility of our planet. Land artists like Andy Goldsworthy and Agnes Denes use natural materials to create installations that emphasize the interconnectedness of humans and nature. Through their work, they aim to inspire a greater appreciation for the environment and promote sustainable practices. Art can serve as a powerful reminder of the importance of preserving our natural world for future generations.

**Political Activism and Protest Art** Artists have also been at the forefront of political activism, using their work to challenge oppressive regimes and advocate for democratic values. In times of political turmoil, protest art can serve as a means of resistance and defiance. The street art of Banksy, for example, often addresses social and political issues, using humor and satire to critique authority and spark conversation. By engaging with political themes, artists can influence public opinion and contribute to the shaping of a more just and equitable society.

**Stories of Art for Social Change** Consider the story of the Guerrilla Girls, an anonymous collective of feminist artists who use visual art to challenge sexism and racism in the art world and beyond. Through provocative posters, performances, and installations, the Guerrilla Girls raise awareness of gender and racial disparities and advocate for greater representation and inclusion. Their work demonstrates the power of art to confront systemic inequalities and drive social change.

# 9

# Chapter 9: The Psychological Impact of Art on the Viewer

Art has the ability to evoke powerful emotions and provoke deep reflection in those who experience it. This chapter delves into the psychological impact of art on the viewer, exploring theories of aesthetic experience and emotional response.

**Theories of Aesthetic Experience** Aesthetic experience refers to the sensory and emotional response we have when encountering a work of art. The philosopher Immanuel Kant argued that aesthetic judgments are based on a feeling of pleasure or displeasure that is free from practical concerns. This idea suggests that our appreciation of art is rooted in a disinterested enjoyment of its beauty and form. Other theorists, such as John Dewey, have emphasized the importance of personal experience and emotional engagement in shaping our aesthetic responses.

**Emotional Response to Art** Art has the power to evoke a wide range of emotions, from joy and awe to sadness and fear. The use of color, composition, and symbolism can influence our emotional response to a work of art. For example, warm colors like red and yellow can evoke feelings of energy and excitement, while cool colors like blue and green can create a sense of calm and tranquility. By tapping into our emotions, artists can create works that resonate on a deeply personal level and provoke meaningful reflection.

## CHAPTER 9: THE PSYCHOLOGICAL IMPACT OF ART ON THE VIEWER

**The Role of Symbolism** Symbolism plays a crucial role in shaping our interpretation of art. Symbols can convey complex ideas and emotions that go beyond the literal meaning of the work. For example, a broken chain might symbolize freedom or liberation, while a stormy sea could represent turmoil and uncertainty. By using symbolic imagery, artists can communicate themes and messages that resonate with viewers on a subconscious level.

**Art as a Mirror of the Self** Viewing art can also be a deeply introspective experience, prompting us to reflect on our own thoughts, feelings, and experiences. Art can serve as a mirror, reflecting aspects of our inner world and revealing truths about ourselves that we may not have been aware of. This introspective quality of art makes it a powerful tool for self-discovery and personal growth. By engaging with art, we can gain insights into our own emotions and experiences, fostering a greater understanding of ourselves and others.

**Stories of Emotional Impact** Consider the story of a viewer who encounters Vincent van Gogh's "Starry Night" for the first time. The swirling patterns and vibrant colors of the painting evoke a sense of wonder and awe, while the melancholic undertones resonate with the viewer's own feelings of longing and introspection. This powerful emotional response demonstrates the ability of art to touch our hearts and minds in profound ways, creating a lasting impact on our perception and experience.

# 10

# Chapter 10: The Artist's Journey: From Inspiration to Creation

The process of creating art is a deeply personal and often arduous journey, filled with moments of inspiration, frustration, and triumph. This chapter explores the artist's journey, from the initial spark of an idea to the final brushstroke or keystroke.

**The Spark of Inspiration** The creative process often begins with a moment of inspiration, a spark that ignites the artist's imagination. This inspiration can come from a variety of sources, such as a fleeting thought, a vivid dream, or a chance encounter with the natural world. For some artists, inspiration strikes like a lightning bolt, while for others, it emerges gradually through reflection and contemplation. Regardless of its origin, this initial spark sets the creative process in motion and provides the motivation to bring the idea to life.

**Brainstorming and Conceptualization** Once the spark of inspiration has been ignited, the artist enters the brainstorming and conceptualization phase. This stage involves generating ideas, exploring different possibilities, and refining the concept. Artists may sketch, write, or engage in other forms of experimentation to develop their vision. This process of exploration allows the artist to clarify their intentions and establish a clear direction for their work.

**Experimentation and Refinement** The journey from inspiration to creation is rarely a straight path. Artists often encounter challenges and obstacles that require them to adapt and experiment with different techniques and approaches. This phase of experimentation and refinement is crucial for honing the work and bringing it closer to the artist's vision. Through trial and error, artists can discover new possibilities and overcome creative blockages.

**The Final Stages of Creation** As the work nears completion, the artist enters the final stages of creation. This phase involves adding the finishing touches, refining details, and ensuring that the work aligns with the artist's vision. The final brushstroke, keystroke, or sculpting motion signifies the culmination of the creative journey and the realization of the artist's idea. This moment of completion can be both exhilarating and bittersweet, as the artist lets go of their creation and shares it with the world.

**Stories of the Creative Process** Consider the story of the painter Claude Monet, who famously created a series of water lily paintings over the course of several decades. Monet's dedication to capturing the ever-changing light and reflections of his garden pond required countless hours of observation, experimentation, and refinement. His journey from inspiration to creation is a testament to the perseverance and passion that drive the artistic process.

**Overcoming Creative Blockages** The creative journey is not without its challenges. Artists often face periods of creative block, where inspiration seems elusive and progress is slow. Overcoming these blockages requires resilience and a willingness to explore new approaches. Some artists find inspiration in nature, others in the works of their peers, and still others through introspection and self-reflection. By embracing the challenges of the creative process, artists can discover new paths and rekindle their creative spark.

**Collaboration and Feedback** While the creative process is often a solitary endeavor, collaboration and feedback from others can play a crucial role in the development of a work of art. Artists may seek input from mentors, peers, or audiences to gain new perspectives and refine their ideas. Constructive feedback can provide valuable insights and help artists overcome creative hurdles. Collaborative projects, where multiple artists contribute to a single work, can also lead to innovative and unexpected results.

**The Emotional Rollercoaster** The journey from inspiration to creation can be an emotional rollercoaster, filled with moments of exhilaration, frustration, doubt, and triumph. The highs of creative breakthroughs are often accompanied by the lows of self-doubt and creative block. By navigating these emotional challenges, artists develop a deeper understanding of themselves and their creative process. This emotional journey is an integral part of the artistic experience, shaping the final work and adding depth and authenticity.

**The Reward of Creation** The completion of a work of art is a moment of profound satisfaction and fulfillment. It is the culmination of the artist's vision, effort, and dedication. Sharing the completed work with others, whether through exhibitions, performances, or publications, allows artists to connect with their audience and make a lasting impact. The reward of creation lies not only in the finished work but also in the journey itself, with all its challenges and triumphs.

# 11

# Chapter 11: The Future of Art and Artistic Expression

As society and technology continue to evolve, so too will the ways in which we express ourselves artistically. This chapter looks ahead to the future of art, exploring emerging trends and potential developments.

**Emerging Art Forms** The future of art will be shaped by emerging forms and mediums that push the boundaries of traditional artistic expression. Virtual reality (VR), augmented reality (AR), and mixed reality (MR) are already transforming the way artists create and interact with their work. These immersive technologies allow for the creation of fully interactive experiences that engage multiple senses and blur the lines between the physical and digital worlds. As these technologies continue to advance, we can expect to see even more innovative and immersive art forms.

**Artificial Intelligence and Machine Learning** Artificial intelligence (AI) and machine learning are poised to revolutionize the art world. AI-powered tools can assist artists in generating new ideas, refining their techniques, and creating complex works that would be difficult to achieve manually. Machine learning algorithms can analyze vast amounts of data to identify patterns and trends, providing artists with new insights and inspiration. The collaboration between human creativity and machine intelligence opens up exciting possibilities for the future of art.

**Sustainability and Eco-Art** As environmental concerns become increasingly urgent, artists are exploring new ways to create sustainable and eco-friendly art. Eco-art, which emphasizes the use of natural materials and environmentally conscious practices, is gaining traction as a movement that promotes environmental awareness and conservation. Artists are experimenting with biodegradable materials, renewable energy sources, and zero-waste production methods to create works that have a positive impact on the planet. By prioritizing sustainability, the future of art can contribute to a more sustainable and eco-conscious world.

**Globalization and Cultural Exchange** Globalization will continue to play a significant role in shaping the future of art. The increasing interconnectedness of the world allows for greater cultural exchange and collaboration, leading to the fusion of diverse artistic traditions and practices. Artists from different cultural backgrounds can draw inspiration from one another, creating work that reflects a global perspective. This cross-cultural exchange enriches the artistic landscape and fosters greater understanding and appreciation of diverse cultures.

**The Role of Technology in Art Preservation** Technology will also play a crucial role in the preservation and dissemination of art. Digital archives, virtual museums, and 3D scanning technologies allow for the preservation of art in digital form, making it accessible to a wider audience and ensuring its longevity. These technologies can also aid in the restoration and conservation of physical artworks, preserving cultural heritage for future generations. By harnessing the power of technology, we can safeguard the legacy of art and ensure its continued impact.

**Imagining the Future** As we look to the future, it is clear that art will continue to evolve in response to societal and technological changes. The fusion of traditional and emerging forms, the collaboration between human and machine, and the emphasis on sustainability and cultural exchange will shape the future of artistic expression. By embracing these trends and innovations, artists can create work that reflects the complexities and wonders of the modern world.

# 12

# Chapter 12: The Eternal Dance of Psychology and Ecology in Art

In the final chapter, we will revisit the central theme of this book: the intricate interplay between psychology and ecology in shaping artistic expression. Through captivating stories of artists who have drawn inspiration from both their inner worlds and their surroundings, we will see how the canvas of the mind is enriched by the vibrant colors of life.

**The Interconnectedness of Mind and Environment** The relationship between psychology and ecology is a dynamic and reciprocal one, with each influencing and shaping the other. Our thoughts, emotions, and experiences are deeply intertwined with our natural surroundings, and this interconnectedness is reflected in the art we create. By understanding this relationship, we can gain a deeper appreciation for the ways in which our minds and environments influence one another.

**Stories of Artistic Inspiration** Consider the story of Emily Carr, a Canadian artist whose work was profoundly influenced by the landscapes and indigenous cultures of the Pacific Northwest. Carr's paintings, which depict the lush forests and totem poles of the region, reflect her deep connection to nature and her appreciation for the cultural heritage of the indigenous peoples. Similarly, the American artist Ansel Adams drew inspiration from the dramatic landscapes of the American West, using his photography to capture the majesty and grandeur of nature.

**The Therapeutic Power of Art** Art can also serve as a powerful tool for healing and personal growth. By engaging with their inner worlds and their natural surroundings, artists can create work that resonates with viewers on a deeply emotional level. The therapeutic power of art lies in its ability to express emotions, tell stories, and connect us to our shared humanity. Through art, we can explore our own experiences and find solace, inspiration, and meaning.

**The Endless Possibilities of Creative Expression** The interplay between psychology and ecology offers endless possibilities for creative expression. Artists can draw on their personal experiences, emotions, and surroundings to create work that is both unique and universal. By embracing the richness and diversity of human experience and the natural world, artists can continue to push the boundaries of artistic expression and inspire others.

**Conclusion: A Celebration of Art** As we conclude our journey through the canvas of the mind, we celebrate the profound connection between art, psychology, and ecology. Through captivating stories, thoughtful reflections, and innovative ideas, we have explored the ways in which our minds and environments shape the art we create. By understanding this dynamic relationship, we can gain a deeper appreciation for the beauty, complexity, and wonder of artistic expression. Art, in all its forms, is a testament to the limitless potential of human creativity and the enduring power of the natural world.

**The Canvas of the Mind: How Psychology and Ecology Shape Artistic Expression**

In "The Canvas of the Mind," readers embark on an enlightening journey through the intricate interplay between psychology, ecology, and artistic expression. This book delves into the depths of the human mind and its connection to the natural world, exploring how these elements influence the creation and appreciation of art.

Across twelve captivating chapters, the book examines the origins of artistic expression, the psychological foundations of creativity, and the profound influence of nature on artistic inspiration. It traces the evolution of artistic techniques and mediums, from prehistoric cave paintings to cutting-edge digital art, and highlights the role of technology in transforming the art world.

Readers will gain insight into how cultural influences shape artistic expression, the intersection of art and science, and the power of art in driving social change. The psychological impact of art on the viewer is explored, revealing how art can evoke powerful emotions and provoke deep reflection. The artist's journey, from inspiration to creation, is brought to life through compelling stories and thoughtful analysis.

Looking ahead, the book imagines the future of art, considering emerging trends such as virtual reality, artificial intelligence, and sustainable art practices. Throughout, "The Canvas of the Mind" celebrates the dynamic relationship between the mind and environment, illustrating how they enrich and inform artistic expression.

Whether you're an artist, art enthusiast, or simply curious about the connections between psychology, ecology, and creativity, "The Canvas of the Mind" offers a thought-provoking and engaging exploration of the boundless possibilities of human creativity and the enduring power of the natural world.

www.ingramcontent.com/pod-product-compliance
Lightning Source LLC
LaVergne TN
LVHW010444070526
838199LV00066B/6195